This book belongs to:

____

Made in the USA
Monee, IL
08 December 2021

84390233R00066